EXPLORING THE ART OF THE
SPIRITUAL ASSESSMENT

A UNIQUE GUIDE EXPLORING AN EMPOWERING
ASPECT OF THE WORK OF AN INTERNATIONAL
PSYCHIC MEDIUM

HELEN DAVITA

For Jac and our children, who gave me the wings to fly, the freedom to follow my vocation and a loving welcome when I returned.

CONTENTS

FOREWORD

Every intuitive/psychic medium will develop their own methodology of the spiritual assessment process. It will become as unique as the sitter they are working with and must be as authentic as their own soul journey. No two assessments will ever be the same.

INTRODUCTION

DISCOVERING THE SPIRITUAL ASSESSOR IN YOU - THE GREAT REVELATION!

The spiritual assessment is a psychic reading (also known as a sitting), primarily conducted for those developing their spiritual abilities and requiring an experienced medium to help them find focus, purpose, validation and empowerment. In the same vein that someone will consult a psychic medium for life guidance, the spiritual assessment will place the emphasis on the spiritual development of the sitter.

The spiritual assessor is an experienced psychic medium, who already understands the terminology described within this book. However, some terms are included in the glossary, as novices practicing for conducting spiritual assessments, may prefer some reference points. Glossary items are underlined.

A sitter requests a spiritual assessment for many different reasons. The most common reasons are:

• Reassurance they are on the right pathway and the next steps

• Feeling 'lost' or 'blocked' with their progress

• Validation of their abilities, experiences and interests

• Discovery of new potentials

• Advice and/or knowledge on how to progress

• Discussion time with an experienced medium

If you are a psychic medium - YOU GOT THIS and it is a liberating way of helping others, through your skills and experience.

For all that you sacrificed and experienced to follow your chosen path, you can now help others, so they are no longer feeling alone, misunderstood and unsupported. The spiritual assessment is the most requested 'one to one' experience at the Arthur Findlay College (The world's foremost college for psychic sciences). Those of us who walk the path of the spirit, know it is a genuine soul journey and also know there are times when we need to take stock of our own progress.

In this book, we will explore the deeper reasons for the spiritual assessment, develop a tried and trusted approach to success for you and your sitter, which empowers and supports each other's goals.

I will also include some genuine 'non identifying' experiences to assist your learning. There is nothing like learning from experience and a good teacher always tells you when they made a mistake and how to avoid it for yourself. I will also share methods and approaches that worked well in my experience.

* * *

PREFACE

In my final year of being assessed to become an 'Approved Tutor' at The Arthur Findlay College, I was to be assessed on the quality of my spiritual assessments. Being assessed is always nerve wracking, but as this was my final year, I was particularly fraught with a fear of failure.

I'd been working for many years as an evidential and psychic medium, before my AFC training, but spiritual assessments were a new format and I was in unfamiliar territory.

My fellow trainees felt the same way and were at a loss as to what to actually do in these 'assessments.' We asked our teaching mentors on that week and had the good fortune to receive excellent advice from the senior tutor - Minister Simone Key. She was an expert in this area and although she did confirm we will all find our own style in time, she gave us her understanding of what it was about and how she conducted them herself.

I remember going to bed and my mind was awash with random ideas about assessments. I had to make this work in my own style, but I also had to fulfil the criteria. A flash of inspiration rushed into my mind, about how this form of 'sitting' was actually very liberating!

Gone was the fear of having to prove anything; such as the importance of accurate evidence of a loved one in spirit. I felt free and excited, to focus on my sitter, their path and offer them my interpretation of their spiritual journey and progress. I felt able to trust this. I knew it would still have to be validated as relevant to the sitter and I could be completely 'off the mark' but the fear dissipated as my excitement grew.

I was particularly inspired by it being a part of a creative, intuitive process, that served the needs of those already with a knowledge of the afterlife and psychic development; yet sought time with someone they felt they could trust.

The path of psychic and evidential mediumship can be lonely. Some find competitiveness, scepticism and criticism hard to cope with and struggle on a personal level. Many on this challenging path give up on their dreams. At times such as this, an experienced assessor can be invaluable in empowering a sitter (or developing spiritual worker) to reflect, celebrate, weigh up the options and make decisions. Taking control of your journey is not just empowering but liberating and confidence building.

The spiritual assessment is a sacred contract between souls. It must be conducted with confidentiality and without ego. The medium's expertise can be measured by the empowerment the sitter receives. It is then down to the sitter to act upon that expertise if they choose.

As a sitter, the assessment is an opportunity to feel that for all the service and giving of the 'self' you have offered to others; the time given to yourself in a spiritual assessment is healing, enlightening, validating, supportive and progressive - but also that this time is now for you.

The hour arrived when my first assessed spiritual assessment of three, would take place. My assessor (none other than Minister Simone Key) took her seat in the corner of the room and I greeted my first sitter. I asked if she had experienced a spiritual assessment before and she looked across at Simone and smiled, turned to me and said "oh yes." I felt intimidated, suddenly filled with fear and in a moment of desperation asked the spirit world and anyone else who was invisible if they could help me and guide me though this. A voice in my mind was yelling "be thorough, be aware of all your senses and follow a path." Follow a path? I decided this must mean a journey with a beginning, middle and conclusion. I had to start and the clock was already counting down.

Three sittings and one and a half hours later, I sat with Simone as she gave me her feedback. I could barely remember a thing about the evening assessments as a result of the relief it was over. The adrenalin had wiped my short term memory. The feedback was that the spiritual assessments were exceptional - just one mistake where I left my timekeeping watch in view of the sitter (not a good look), but otherwise exceptional!

I was of course delighted and over the next few days the sitters kept coming to me asking where and when I'd be working next and relaying parts of their assessments (which I still had no memory of).

Over the next 10 years I set about exploring the processes of the spiritual assessment. There was not one set magical formula, that would work for everyone. How could there be? Each sitter and their journey is unique. Some prefer a general assessment whilst others need a specific focus. I have even experienced several who just sat down and talked for 30 minutes - wouldn't let me get a word in edgeways and then left stating they now had a clear idea of how to progress! There is no 'one size' fits all and clearly, just the intention is sometimes enough for some.

However, for learning and developing your own style of spiritual assessment, there are a number of areas to consider - adopt if you wish, expand and incorporate. With this in mind, I have written and developed this guide.

With your knowledge and experience I am sure that a spiritual assessment, delivered from the heart with the power of a genuinely positive intention, will become magical possibilities & potentials for others following their spiritual pathway.

We have good work to do!

INSIGHTS OF THE SPIRITUAL ASSESSMENT

The professional spiritual assessment is a psychic and intuitive reading, to assist both the experienced and the developing spiritual worker. It can help us understand:

• Insights of the individual spiritual path

• Discover, revisit, confirm and celebrate their strengths and potentials

• Recommended training, education and relevant professional development

Every professional and developing spiritual worker encounters the so called 'blocks'. It is at these times we search the soul for insight. Yet these blocks can be difficult to overcome when we are actively engaged, or even feeling 'stuck' with our work. Being able to spend some time with a professional who is skilled at exploring your pathway, helps to consolidate your own journey, empowers you to discover solutions to move forward and validates your work and progress.

.   .   .

If the assessment is conducted professionally and positively, the 'sitter' should leave with a sense of pride, acknowledgement and a positive mental action plan, to push through the 'blocks' and further their progress.

This progress will encourage most sitters to move forward with their own spiritual work. Some will find that their assessment may be a time to help them decide to take a break - to regroup and renew for now. Others will find their 'aha' moments and leave feeling renewed and ready to move forward. In all cases, a professional spiritual assessment should enlighten and empower.

Insights of the individual spiritual path

It is such an individual process that the outcomes may come as surprises to the sitter. For example, one lady came to me 10 years ago, for an assessment when I was working as the Course Leader at the Arthur Findlay College. I had known her for some years and taught her many times. Her mediumship was going very well and her work was in great demand in the USA. It would appear she had nothing to be concerned about. Sometimes the assessment is purely a reassurance of that. However, in her case she just knew something was amiss.

As I explored her energy and my psychic senses worked with her, I was intentionally working on her present spiritual energy. A mental image flashed in my mind of her writing a book and I was clairvoyantly shown the image of her sitting back, just staring at the blank pages. I sensed this was a project she was committed to; but that she felt she had a writer's block.

.   .   .

I described what I had seen; I explained this all to her and what I sensed it all meant. She smiled and laughed and said "yes it's driving me nuts" I keep putting it off - it's like the film 'Groundhog Day' where I repeat the same thing each day. Every morning I wake up intending to write and then I always tell myself 'later - do it later' - by which time the day has passed and I'm just too tired to write.

I asked her if I could take a moment - to focus on this in order to discover a way forward. As soon as I set the intention to focus, an image of a tropical beach flashed through my mind and she was writing on the wooden veranda overlooking the ocean. She looked healthy, happy and relaxed.

As I relayed this vision, I explained that to move forward she needed to find a place that would bring her both wellness and peace and was miles away from her usual routine and home-life.

Her reply astounded me. The day before her assessment with me, her dearest friend had offered her the use of her beach house for as long as she needed it. It was in Maui - overlooking the ocean! It hadn't occurred to her that this was her opportunity to write that book. To change the routine and focus on an important aspect of her life - plus she always felt healthy and relaxed near the ocean.

Fast forward three years and she returned to the college and booked another assessment with me. I was so delighted that she had gone to Maui, written her book and was returning to write the 3rd one in a couple of months' time! What also occurred was that after publishing her first book, her own spiritual work took on a new dimension, and she began teaching others to develop their spiritual healing path. This new direction was bringing her great happiness

3

in life and all aspects of her development were extremely satisfying and progressing very well for her.

This is just one example of the thousands of spiritual assessments that I have conducted personally, but what it shows is that no matter how skilled we are; having another professional evaluate, sense and share what they discover is 'within and around' the sitter, enables a positive boost to their progress.

It can sometimes be too difficult to see the wondrous possibilities available to us, when we are engaged in our usual routines, experiences and expectations. A well conducted spiritual assessment can ensure the sitter has a pathway to progress - including when the best outcome is to do nothing, in the immediate future.

Discover, revisit, confirm & celebrate their strengths and potentials

As part of the spiritual assessment, the medium can explore the past, the present and potential outcomes for the sitter's development. The path of spiritual development is often first noted by memories of childhood spiritual experiences. Sometimes, it is explained as having imaginary friends! However, there may also be memories of significant events recalled, such as seeing and speaking to deceased loved ones, that they could not have met in their childhood.

Healers were often the children, frequently playing 'doctors and nurses' and animal communicators displayed tremendous empathy and kinship with animals. Seeing clairvoyantly both objectively and subjectively are common experiences of childhood, along with clairaudience.

If we can 'tap into' the formative experiences and offer validated examples, the sitter grows in confidence that their chosen pathway was important to them from the outset.

Not everyone began their pathway in their formative years. For many, it is a discovery made later in life. This could mean they have simply forgotten or not attached a significance to early spiritual experiences. Or, it is possible that the catalyst for spiritual awareness just happened to 'steam' in later in life. Earlier or later is not as important, as the medium identifying the first stirrings of spiritual awareness and validating this for the sitter.

The skills to explore the energy of the sitter and confirm their abilities is key to the successful spiritual assessment. It will not only validate the work of the sitter, but is often a great healing tool. Far too often I meet sitters who have valuable spiritual work to do, yet their confidence has been eroded by a thoughtless and unskilled teacher/relative/friend, undermining them. When the medium confirms the skills that are present, latent and ripe for further development, the sitter rediscovers the significance of all they have been working towards and regains their confidence. This aspect is highly rewarding for both sitter and medium.

Latent and potential considerations for spiritual development are extremely interesting. Identifying new areas is exciting and offers the sitter areas of previously unexplored thought.

Spiritual progress is the exploration of many aspects and sometimes, planting the seeds of emerging or forgotten areas, leads to new and exciting directions. Every avenue explored is a magical pathway that adds value to a sitter's wholeness of spiritual progress. Ultimately, the sitter decides whether to embrace the new or undiscovered areas of development.

It is not unusual to see a sitter years later, after a spiritual assessment, who showed no interest in a specific area of development, that the medium had explored; yet later embraces it with a grand passion. We can plant the seeds from what we sense, but the power to act is always in the hands and hearts of the sitters.

Training, education and relevant professional development

Exploring the past or current methods of development for any sitter may yield interesting results. Specifically, I am referring to any relevant courses, spiritual teachers, self - education, spiritual guides mentors, etc. Once again, validation is helpful and reassuring. It can instil a sense of confidence in a sitter who is feeling lost, when they realise just how much knowledge they have gained, what they achieved and also explored.

Even occasions when a course or a teacher appears to have been a negative experience for the sitter, adds to the overall assessment accuracy and can lead to discovering what they learned and why it was important to move on. As long as we find a forward direction for the sitter, it is a valuable aspect to explore.

Recommending new or specialist teachers, courses, books and spiritual exercises is valuable to the sitter and also, the medium is showing a greater awareness of the opportunities available to the sitter.

It is good practice to introduce future training and development opportunities at the end of an assessment, so it empowers the sitter to take action if appropriate and if they choose.

Unscrupulous teaching mediums may use this opportunity to self promote their services. A good spiritual assessor will offer a range of options. It may be that the sitter chose their assessor as they wish to know more about their services and whether they 'fit' with their ideals. This must come from the sitter first if invited, rather than any blatant self -promotion.

Therefore, in studying the practice of the spiritual assessment, we commit firstly to the sitter who has put their trust in us and honour the commitment to assist them with integrity.

Exercise: Take some time to write or record your first memories of spiritual awareness. Then write down all the books you read, the films that impacted you and any courses and teachers who left a lasting impression and why.

* * *

SKILLS & ATTRIBUTES OF THE
SPIRITUAL ASSESSOR

SKILLS & ATTRIBUTES

There are many attributes and skills required by a competent spiritual assessor and these include:

• capacity for 'attunement' & intention

• has developed their own psychic faculties

• awareness of the different spiritual energies & abilities presented by their sitter.

• able to remain objective, realistic, positive and non judgemental

Being able to explore specific areas of development, rather than a general overview is important - as is the ability to offer a plan of progress with sound advice, tailored to the individual sitter.

Attunement

Attunement relates to a state of energetic spiritual harmony. It is in this state where we feel a sense of being 'at one' with either a higher power, another person, animal or nature, or even a sense of completeness with our own spirit and soul.

Moments of attunement are very special and leave us feeling gratitude and wonder. Yet in our attunement, we can achieve a great deal relating to spiritual assessments. For once we are attuned to the person we are assessing, our own intuitive and psychic senses reveal the puzzles, the solutions, the abilities and also the journey the sitter may have taken and be currently travelling along.

If you have ever experienced moments of feeling totally 'connected' to either someone, a place, another animal, or a total 'peace' within yourself - you are in a state of attunement - you are in harmony.

"I stand atop the mountain

Powerful gusts pull my roots,

Unexpected, complete - we could not separate - we depended on each other, in one battle"

The opposite of attunement is a feeling of disconnection and may create barriers to the state of being in harmony. It creates a separation. However, feeling separation can often be a choice for some and is how they may feel content or in their comfort zone. Not everyone wants or needs to feel connected and harmonious. For others, their experience, upbringing or relationships may influence their need for separation and it is also possible to be both separatist and in harmony, depending on the situation.

We are complex beings, and it is impossible to be in a permanent state of harmony with everything all the time. This is a clue as to why an experienced spiritual worker and student may need a spiritual assessment - they may no longer feel attuned to their work and development. They have a sense of feeling lost.

Achieving attunement for spiritual assessments is undertaken through different methods. You will find what works the best for you over time. As the assessor, you may either know what already works for you, or perhaps you wish to explore and experiment with other methods too. Either way, the choice is yours and what follows are some tried and trusted methods. In fact, the more you try different approaches, the greater your capacity to discover how your sitter has been working and what may be the best way forward for them. It's a win - win; so enjoy experimenting and what doesn't work now - may become a future possibility.

However, to activate attunement you need the power of intention.

Intention

The greatest force of attunement begins with the power of intention. When intention is activated, the attunement process has started very positively.

'The power of intention, is critical for spiritual work. With intention, we're not really talking about what we normally understand as intention. So the word intention implies an aim or a plan. In your spiritual assessments, psychic work, mediumship, (whether it be demonstrating publicly, one-to-one sittings, assessments or healing) or whether you're using your intention for any other spiritual discipline - what's critical is not that you want it to be a certain outcome, it's that you actually feel it is.

When you feel it, your energy shifts, something really important happens within you. It's not just a case of, I want to sit down conduct an amazing spiritual assessment and it's going to happen. You have to actually feel as if you are in that energy, in that power, because what's really happening here is we're talking about working with emotional energy. And when we're in the right emotional energy, it's the law of attraction weaving its magic. Like attracts like. We're wanting to work with an emotional subject in a practical way. If we're in the wrong emotion, we're just not going to attract what we need to know to help our sitter. So intention becomes a point of attraction and to achieve it, you have to feel it within yourself.

But let's look at it another way, just for a moment. I'm being a little cheeky here. If I were to say to you "go and buy a bunch of bananas" you're not going to go to a computer hardware store. You want your bananas, so you're going to go to the supermarket, or you're going to go to the grocery store or wherever sells them. With spiritual assessments and intention, it's the same principle. You're not going to just sit and say, right, I'm going to give you a great assessment and hope it just happens. You have to feel you're in that power, you have to feel you're capable, you have to feel as if you are a spirit, and you're ready. You have to go to the right place - but this time you go to a place that is within you.

There are lots of ways of creating an intention, with using the power of the mind. It's not a want. It is a state of being. To be it, feel it, think it. Imagination is the most powerful thing. Nobody can take away your thoughts. Nobody knows where a thought comes from. Nobody knows where thought really goes. Nobody can change what you think. And so if you think it, you can also feel it,

11

you will change your power - and that will be your point of attraction.

When you set your intention for a spiritual assessment, allow your mind to take you to a special invisible place, where you and your sitter are totally happy together and harmonious - where the flow of information is exciting and exact. Do this just before you meet and the intention is ready to go to work. That's your point of attraction for each other and it starts here with the power of intention.

Now it is time to move on to the next stage - attunement.

Further Methods Of Attunement

For some, experience and practice will ensure that just setting the intention will enable attunement. They have so much experience working with psychic energy, that it's almost as if they can 'flip' a switch in the mind and they are good to go.

However, even if you attune very quickly, your sitter deserves the best outcome and a little time, spent on a dedicated attunement process and focus will usually improve the outcome of any assessment.

Having set the intention here are some methods that can assist a deeper attunement for the spiritual assessment:

• mindfulness

• breath work

• visualisation

Mindfulness

Mindfulness is a form of meditation in which the participant observes the thoughts that arise, acknowledges them and lets them go from the mind. We can also practice mindfulness with a specific purpose, such as:

Compassion

Forgiveness

Love

Letting go of the past

Or we can simply sit and focus on whatever thoughts arise. Whether you have a theme or it is a random mindfulness exercise, the solution is to acknowledge each thought or theme, observe what arises from it and then to let it go. Key to this is not engaging and suffering. For example; suppose I want to let go of a painful memory of a relationship breakup. I can sit close my eyes, relax my body and focus on my breath for a while. Then I introduce the idea of the failed relationship. I observe it in my mind how I feel. I am observing, not participating. However, I also observe that it causes me some tension in the solar plexus area. So I note that, but don't engage with it. I stay in control. I tell myself that a certain kind of stress; I feel it in the solar plexus. Such an experience puts me back in control of my emotions and how they can affect me. This empowers me and may feel I don't have to suffer this situation anymore, as I can observe and not participate.

. . .

That is a simple explanation, but mindfulness is actually very easy and effective. If this is for you, it is worth studying.

Breathwork

In many eastern practices, breath work is paramount. In fact, the word 'spirit' is derived from meaning 'breath' - to inspire. When we focus on the breath, we are no longer within our own busy mind. There are countless breathing exercises to try and its important to only try as far as it is comfortable. As an example, I would teach students who were demonstrating mediumship publicly the technique of inhaling to a count of 4 and exhaling to a count of 8. If they did this prior to demonstrating, it would settle their nerves. I found it worked well for me and for most of them too.

Even if it's it's merely a case of mind distraction, breath work has many benefits. Our status quo is to not even take any notice of the breath. When we focus, we tend to breathe well - that is we inhale properly and fully throughout the lungs; not just the top 1/3 of each lobe. If you watch a healthy newborn breathing, you can observe the belly rising and falling. It inhales fully. As we age and our posture changes, we tend not to inflate the lungs properly. Therefore, breath work has benefits beyond focus - it supports our well being too.

An animal communication student of mine posted the following from the book 'Inner Engineering' Sadhguru:

What is the significance of slowing down the human breath? Is it just some respiratory yogic acrobatics? No, it is not. A human being breathes twelve to fifteen times per minute, normally. If your breath settles down to twelve, you will know the ways of the earth's atmosphere (i.e., you will become meteorologically sensitive). If it reduces to nine, you will know the language of the other creatures on this planet. If it reduces to six, you will know the very language of the earth. If it reduces to three, you will know the language of the source of creation. This is not about increasing your aerobic capacity. Nor is it about forcefully depriving yourself of breath. A combination of hatha yoga and an advanced yogic practice called the kriya, will gradually increase your lung capacity, but above all, will help you achieve a certain alignment, a certain ease, so that your system evolves to a state of stability where there is no static, no crackle; it just perceives everything.

As Sadhguru states 'it perceives everything' - which is what we need in our assessments. Also note, where he highlighted that a breath count of 9 per minute, is the level to know the language of other creatures. We humans are creatures too.

If you haven't practised breath work before, start off with a comfortable level such as:

Exercise: Ensure you are sat upright, with no restrictive clothing. Inhale for a count of 3 - exhale for a count of three - hold for a count of 3, repeating this breath pattern. Do this at a gentle, comfortable pace for around 30 seconds to start. Then return to your normal pace. If you discover breath work is effective for you to attune, then there are many original books, courses, free videos and traditions available. However, a good teacher and course has no substitute. Their shared wisdom and experience, ensures you will get the most from breath techniques, if you discover this is helpful for you.

Visualisation

Visualisation is a mentally active technique that is effective for some people. When we work with the psychic faculty, we are engaging our senses and that stimulates brain activity.

Another way to consider this is in terms of software and hardware. The consciousness of thought and the emotional energy present in all of us is the software - it gives the instructions to the brain. The complex brain that processes the software may then show us images, or activate the autonomic system so we get 'goose bumps' in response to an emotional thought. They are interdependent. The theory is such that when the body dies, the software is the part of us that is the eternal intelligence.

To visualise is to have a thought and let the brain process the information for us, so it makes sense as a picture, symbol, scene, colour, etc.

As an example for a spiritual assessment, we could visualise the medium and the sitter in a bubble together, or even a plain room with no distractions. As we have this thought, the brain shows us a representation. Mentally we become prepared for the sitting as being a special time for just the two of us and a positive experience. It has become familiar already. This also underpins the importance of the intention aspect too.

Furthermore, we have engaged the visual area of the physical brain and in doing so primed it for any information to be received as mental images. Consider it a warmup to the major exercise!

Mindfulness, breath work and visualisation are just three methods to assist attunement. You may have your own way or wish to explore further, but within these three methods - or even a combination, you may find attunement can be enhanced significantly and will also help you to know that you are truly engaging with the sitter.

* * *

THE PSYCHIC FACULTIES

THE PSYCHIC FACULTIES

THE PSYCHIC FACULTIES

Having set your intention, attuned to the sitter and decided between you the purpose of the spiritual assessment, your psychic faculties are ready to go to work. The most common forms of psychic awareness are experienced as:

• Clairvoyance (seeing images)

• Clairaudience (hearing sounds or words)

• Clairsentience (sensing information)

• Claircognisance (a sense of 'knowing' something)

Other awarenesses may be experienced as:

. . .

- Tastes

- Scents

- Physical sensations (such as tingling)

All of these experiences are known as mental mediumship, as the mind is working hard to interpret information for you.

You may experience all these psychic faculties as being within the mind, yet at times, they appear physical experiences. They are all phenomena of the mind, no matter how 'real' they seem. Yet your body may also react to them. For example, sensing an unpleasant scent or taste may lead you to feeling physically nauseous. A powerful emotion may cause you to be feeling a lump in your throat. A tingling sensation may result in you wanting to scratch it. However, it is all mental mediumship.

In essence, with mental mediumship we could say that it is all classed as clairsentience:

- We sense the image in our mind

- We sense a sound

- We sense a taste or scent, etc

- We sense information

However, we can discern how the experience is manifesting in the mind by the individual terms and thus, we make the distinctions.

* * *

SPIRITUAL ENERGIES, THE AURIC FIELD, ABILITIES & POTENTIALS

SPIRITUAL ENERGIES, THE AURIC FIELD

Everyone we meet has arrived in this world with a soul purpose. Whether that is realised or not is something for the individual to discover. Yet, the role of the medium can be particularly helpful here.

Although we cannot take the same pathway as our sitter, we may become aware of several qualities, abilities and potentials within their energy field. By the energy field I am referring to the 'aura'.

The Aura is the electromagnetic energy field that surrounds us and is constantly expressing our state of being in response to our energy. It emanates from within us and also externally and is influenced by our health, our mood, our connection to spirituality, our guides, what we are thinking, how we behave etc.

We tend to think of the aura as multi-layered, when it is actually a dynamic force of interrelated energies, merging, moving and reacting to both the spiritual and physical worlds and our thoughts.

Some may see the aura through their clairvoyant ability, whilst others sense or just have a knowing. Each aspect of the aura is often represented by a colour. Each colour is a frequency and also corresponds to the internal energy centres called 'Chakras.' This is clearly a complex system, and those who work with colour energy are accustomed to discovering information with their skills and knowledge.

Whether you feel confident to read an aura or whether you are unsure, what really matters is that when the sitter presents for a spiritual assessment, (either on a conscious or subconscious level), you are aware their energy may influence your first impression. We will look at the first impression in more detail in a forthcoming chapter. For now; our awareness of a new sitter's energy is expressed energetically through their aura and your acceptance of this will be a route to their needs.

Our job as assessors is to discover as much as we can, that will empower the sitter to move forward on their path of development. The energies present will reveal many possibilities, abilities, hopes and dreams. You may not be one who ever sees auras, but as mediums you understand energy and that energy is your navigation through the assessment.

You will need to be aware of all our own 'Clair' senses and when they are working for you, to recognise them in others. We need to have a good understanding of what possibilities are available and which ones are dominant, latent and require nurturing in the sitter's energy.

Next we consider aspects you may encounter and should have an awareness of. Some have been mentioned previously, but a visual chart is helpful (the contents are not exhaustive and do feel free to add your own if you can't find something here).

* * *

ABILITIES, INTERESTS & POTENTIALS

General Categories of Mediumship

The field of spiritual development and accompanying disciplines is vast and the need to have as much awareness as possible will make more sense in your assessments, when presented with psychic impressions from your sitter. Have a look at some of them below and also create your own map - adding more:

With every ability, interest or potential that you become aware of in an assessment, there is an opportunity for expansion. Every concept leads to others and it soon becomes a web of connections and potential for depth of the subject itself. Lets look at trance as an example:

- How long in development?
- What trance aspects interest the sitter?
- Any challenges?
- How to take it to another level?

The list has so many possibilities that simply discovering an interest in trance leads to so much more.

 If you think of every piece of information as part of web of connections, you will never be stuck for how to delve into a sitter's development.

Exercise: With pen and paper or a voice recorder, write down or record one spiritual skill you work with (e.g trance, healing, tarot, demonstrating, meditation etc.. Now answer the following questions, either on paper or by recording (As you note your responses, also write down any images, colours, emotions, sensations or new thoughts that accompany your answers.):

- When did I start noticing I could do this?
- How does it make me feel?
- What sources of education helped me?
- Who do I respect, who also does this now?
- What challenges have I faced in developing it?
- How did I overcome the challenges?
- What would I need to do to take it to the next stage?
- What can I do in the next three months to improve my skills?

Whatever spiritual skill you noted, by answering these questions you will discover a web of connected information, you can delve into. This web gives you a more complete assessment and you can use this approach in your professional assessments with others.

Over time, this expansion on a subject becomes second nature and becomes organic . You will find yourself naturally following the connections as you work, without having to think about them.

* * *

THE SPACE FOR THE IDEAL ASSESSMENT

ONLINE ASSESSMENTS

T oday we have more ways than ever to conduct spiritual assessments. The online world is available to many and ensures that we don't have to travel long distances.

 Although many still prefer the 'in person' assessment, there is no barrier to sensing the energy of someone and psychically attuning to them online. Energy is energy and although we can sense atmospheres and changes in a room, it is possible to sense perfectly well through the medium of technology. Here are some points to consider when working online:

1. Video: – You don't need to have the best video camera, phone, tablet or webcam – good lighting is the biggest factor to producing a good quality image.

2. Add light if required (it almost always is needed): the effect of poor lighting is grainy video image quality. Use lights facing you to add more, but by all means avoid ring lights if possible. I know they are cheap and portable but.....

Ring lights have this weird effect that makes you look weird – it gives you alien eyes.

Soft diffuse light works best, but also use daylight wisely, if video teaching during the day. Filming with a window behind you turns you into a silhouette – a faceless figure with a piercing glare behind you. Let natural light enter by facing you for best effect. If you need to add lights ensure the light falls evenly on both sides your face, to prevent shadows.

If you wear glasses like me – you can invest in anti glare lens coatings which will help reduce distracting reflections.

3. Good audio is critical. If the sound is poor – no matter how engaging you are, everyone just focusses on the fact that the sound is poor, gets irritated and ignores your valuable wisdom. If your microphone is built in to your computer, phone, tablet – it might be really good and no need to add anything extra. Check it out with a friend online.

Lavalier mics (lapel) and desktops mics are also worth considering if the built in mic happens to be poor, but your room is key to good sound production. A room with plenty of soft furnishings and without machines running in the background will dampen any hollow sounding effects. Add some cushions around you and in front of you (out of camera sight) to help if the room is bare of soft furnishings. Professional studios are awash with sound dampening panels and flooring – but you can do a decent job with a few home furnishings, to capture the warmth in your voice.

4. Internet speed makes a wealth of difference. Most important is the upload speed. Anything less than 5 Mbps upload, will often result in the 'spinny buffering wheel of doom' stuttering speech and blurry pixelations. You can test your internet speed here at speeedtest.net

5. Turn off any computer or phone notifications. There's nothing worse than hearing that familiar 'bing' and all your students checking if it's them – and from the get-go tell them to turn theirs off too while you are at it.

6. Your background shouldn't be distracting. A natural background is great. I'm sure your room is great too. However, if you are in the bedroom, home office or kitchen, hide the dirty pots, laundry, bins, paper collection and unmade bed with either a screen, a fake background or changing your position to having a wall behind you.

Talking fake backgrounds – we see many using them on zoom and other online platforms and some look great – until the person moves and leaves a distracting pixel trail around them. If you use them, a plain background behind you before selecting the fake one, is kindest and prevents the distraction of your students all thinking "hey thats a fake background – I wonder what the room really looks like and what did they just say?"

You can use a green screen if you wish but the screen needs to be very good quality, it must be extremely evenly lit, or else it is just as unforgiving as the 'pixel creep' in a fake zoom background. Just don't wear green clothes if you do, or you will look as if you are wearing Harry Potter's invisibility cloak!

Here's a mini tip if you want to use a background and you are seated – sit on a chair with no arms and the back height lower than your shoulders – it really helps prevent the dreaded pixel creep, as the sensor calibrates around you when you are sitting still. The moment you move, a new colour and texture makes it throw a pixel wobbly and spoils the overall effect.

7. Body positioning can make or break how professional your online class appears. Ideally you want to be central like a newsreader. Sitting upright is important. If you slump back – your body looks huge, your head looks tiny and frankly, you look unmotivated. Sitting upright and slightly forward is ideal. some experts say an angle of 15 degrees forward is best, but I've not worked out how to effectively measure my body angle yet! Trial and error are great friends to prepare with prior to teaching.

8. Camera positioning is vital so you can be central and is good at approximately 2 inches above your eye-line. Too high looks just weird....

Too low and we are distracted by your nostrils!

Yes I know she looks great in this photo, but the first thing I see are her **nostrils!**

You might also find it difficult if using a laptop, to find the right height – but a pile of books underneath is excellent as a prop, if you don't have an adjustable stand and nobody can see them.

Look at the camera and not the computer screen. It's hard, I know but will make such a difference and actually your students will feel you are talking directly to them. Which you are, but at least it will look as if you are too.

9. Your voice is your asset. Use it with varying emphasis, pitch, tone

and pace. Remember the teacher who you never forgot for their wise advice? – that advice was most likely said slowly, calmly and with intent for impact.

Volume for your delivery should be normal and there is no need to project your voice online. It will only create a strain on your students ears, kills your microphone, distorts your voice and is unnatural. With good eye contact and a normal volume, your students will feel much more compelled to learn with you.

10. Know your subject thoroughly. You just might have an experienced sitter in the online room who knows far more than you and in one reasonable Q&A, will leave your credibility in tatters. Your sitters deserve to be assessed by an expert and not someone with a smidgen of knowledge.

11. Confidentiality is paramount. Ensure you and your sitters know that it is unacceptable that non participants in the household could see or hear the sitting and that it breaches the trust of the students who cant see them and may wish to share something personal with you. It may be online but a spiritual assessment needs a sacred, private space.

12. Know the class platform inside out. Zoom, Skype and even live feed classes, all have a zillion 'how to' training videos online and on

YouTube and are a great investment to the smooth running of your class.

13. It's stating the obvious – but if you have no training – do it before launching your service and calling yourself a spiritual assessor. There are plenty of sources including this book, if you cant go in person.

14. Have a 'plan B' in case you get a powercut or technology failure and let your students know what plan B is in advance of the class.

15. Be user friendly – if you record the session for student download – add subtitles. Here is some great software I use for all my videos called Otter. It's very accurate and you can find it here

16. Lastly – as thats enough for now, look like an authority . It's ok that nobody can see your slippers or odd coloured socks – but ensure that what they do see is someone who has taken some care before showing up to teach. It doesn't have to be formal attire – just appropriate and nothing distracting. Psychologically it shows you care and take the students and subject seriously.

17. To record or not to record? Recording online can be valuable as it is a record of the assessment, the student won't take in everything you have said and will enjoy watching it back. However, there must be confidentiality and the risk of your work being shared to others is real. Do ensure your sitter states clearly they will not share the recording without your permission. Ideally ask them to confirm this whilst being recorded and before you start the assessment.

There may be issues with data protection, so check out in your country what the laws are and what counts as safe storage of recordings.

There is skill to assessing well and online is here to stay now. If you are thinking about it, these tips may help save you time and ensure your professionalism remains intact.

IN PERSON SPIRITUAL ASSESSMENTS

There have many occasions when I have conducted a spiritual assessment in a less than ideal location or situations.

You would imagine that the library at the Arthur Findlay College would be perfect and often it is. However, it is sometimes too cold, too hot and the gardeners are cutting the grass outside and making a lot of noise. This can and does happen and if you have the choice, find the quietest room where nobody in the building has to enter to get to the bathroom through it etc.

Choose somewhere if possible that is accessible to all. Years ago I lived in a lovely house that had 16 steps up to the front door. I was younger and fitter then and it didn't occur to me it would be an issue, until a lady with a damaged hip arrived at my front door in a lot of pain. At that point I made sure that anyone who booked, knew about the steps.

Room temperature and cleanliness are important and in particular pets. Allergy sufferers often ask in advance, but if you do have pets, please ensure the room is either barred from them, or is thoroughly clean of dust and pet allergens.

The chairs need to be comfortable but not too comfortable (having extra cushions available can help for anyone with back issues). On one occasion, a lady sat down on my sofa and mentioned how nice it was. We had just bought it. Without thinking I said it was a recliner so it was relaxing for us to put our feet up. With that she pulled the recliner lever and laid back - completely flat, closed her eyes and instructed me to continue. It was so distracting and I kept wondering if she had fallen asleep. At the end of the assessment she arose and said she had barely taken anything in as she was too relaxed!

I always have fresh water and tissues at hand. No matter how positive you are the subject of development is often emotional and often in a good way. The water is not only good manners and considerate, but it is also ideal if someone arrives feeling stressed. Perhaps they were stuck in traffic or as sometimes happens - they forgot, then turned up late and very anxious. As you settle them in with some light conversation, the offer of a sip of water can help significantly.

WRITTEN ASSESSMENTS

Email and letter assessments can be another method of delivery and some people love the printed format to keep and look back to in years to come. Ideally, ensure before you begin that you won't be distracted and that you know if the assessment is a general one, or has a specific theme to explore. Again ensure any copies are kept in accordance with data protection laws in your country.

I've conducted spiritual assessments in many locations including:

- On a rowing boat on a lake
- On top of a mountain
- In a forest
- A stately home for members of the royal family
- A church toilet!
- At 38,000 ft on a plane

Some places are not ideal or conducive, but it demonstrates that where there is a will there is a way!

* * *

THE INITIAL EXPLORATION OF A
SPIRITUAL ASSESSMENT

A great way to start an assessment is to ask at the beginning of the assessment "Is there a specific area of your development you would like me to focus on?" This is very important. Many sitters who arrive and when asked, will merely reply that they just want to see what arises from the medium's perceptions. Yet, it is common at the end of a productive assessment for the sitter to state something more specific, when time is about to run out. For example:

Peter came to me in the library of the Arthur Findlay College and arrived promptly for his assessment. As he sat down, took a sip from his water bottle, I welcomed him to his assessment and to ease the conversation, made some small talk about the beautiful room we were in - surrounded by many first edition books on Spiritualism.

I then asked him if he knew what a spiritual assessment was, and he said he wasn't really sure. I explained it was an intuitive reading focusing on his spiritual pathway and associated interests, abilities, activities and any related issues he wished me to explore with him. This was met with a big smile and nod of approval. I then asked him if he had anything specific in mind that he would like me to explore as well . "Not really" he replied. "I admire your work and anything you discover will give me something to work with."

This could have appeared quite flattering, but my focus was to ensure Pete felt his work and his interests were validated and that he would feel empowered with some clear future goals.

The assessment duration was for 30 minutes and was conducted as a general assessment; where I explored as many areas as possible. I discovered his love of trance healing in particular, and a growing interest in physical mediumship. Pete was smiling and nodding all the way through. It appeared it had gone very well.

37

. . .

In the last few minutes of each assessment, I always ask if there is anything important the sitter would like to ask me, that hasn't been mentioned so far, or has arisen from something I had mentioned. Peter told me that I had been 'spot on' with everything, but he was confused about which trance healing teachers would suit him. We were pushed for time by then, but I managed to give him some information - although it was unfortunately rushed.

If you are clear about - "Is there a specific area of your development you would like me to focus on?" There is a greater possibility that we can apportion the most pressing issues with greater time and depth.

The moral is that as responsible mediums, we can know the motivations for someone booking a spiritual assessment and we must be clear, within the timeframe and scope of enquiry, what the most important issue is to the sitter and that some quality time is given for this.

Tips:

• Be clear about what a spiritual assessment can offer

• Ask if the sitter has any expectations, or special areas of interest

• Leave time for questions, clarifications, and anything that arisen from the assessment

CHALLENGES

COPING WITH CHALLENGES

An aspect which is liberating with the spiritual assessment, is that it's difficult to get it wrong. What I mean by this, is that what you genuinely sense, will usually have some basis of truth. The danger and temptation for the struggling medium, is to become general in the information they read from the sitter. However, if you stick to what you genuinely sense through your psychic ability, the chances are it will be relevant to the sitter.

CONFUSING INFORMATION

Sometimes, the information that the medium receives is opposite to the initial interpretation. As an example, I kept sensing that my sitter was skilled and interested in spiritual art. When I mentioned this, they gave me a very definite 'no.' Yet the information was so clear to me. I had seen a clairvoyant image of her drawing faces and working alongside a well-known demonstrating medium. The two appeared to be working together, and it seemed clear to me it was genuine.

The temptation is that what you receive as a medium in an assessment is always positive or on face value–as it appears to you literally. In this case, the sitter was highly skilled at portrait drawings, but had no interest to work this way. The well-known demonstrating medium had been encouraging them to work with them publicly, but the sitter had no desire to do so. This had actually caused the sitter to be stressed.

This was a clear example of how, as a medium conducting an assessment, you need to be aware of how information and energy presents and also feels. In this case, the image I saw was very positive, yet if I had taken a little more time to analyse it, I'd have also sensed the resistance that was there from the sitter. Once the sitter corrected me, I had the 'aha' moment because I remembered something didn't feel quite right about it all.

Therefore, whatever you receive as a medium, self-check it, with how it feels. Could it be:

- True

- Positive

- Exciting

- Frustrating

- The worst thing for the sitter

Often you will be given significant information, but it must be double checked whether this could be a rejected potential or a troublesome issue, and also the possibility it is positive. We can never take it for granted that everything is wonderful for the sitter.

Exercise: Some mediums combine a traffic light system, along with their emotional senses, for exploring the information they receive. Green for go – amber for caution and of course red is a no-go area.

A simple exercise is to practice yourself with foods. Sit quietly, close your eyes and think of foods you love. Visualise the green traffic light but also notice how you feel. Commit that feeling and/or the green light in your mind to your memory. Repeat this exercise for foods you are ambivalent about and also foods you dislike. Over time, you will gain confidence how the information relates to your sitter's ideals.

SETTING LIMITATIONS AND COPING WITH DISAPPOINTMENTS

The importance of explaining exactly what a sitter can expect, the timeframe and the purpose of the assessment, cannot be overstressed. In fact, it will save a lot of confusion and sometimes distress if the sitter is clear on the objectives at the outset.

I would go so far as to say that as long as you leave enough time near the end for questions, you shouldn't expect the sitter to request several follow up emails, messages or visits.

You may be asked – when should I book another assessment? This will depend on what has transpired during the sitting, but also it should allow for any actions recommended to be put into practice first. A usual time span is 6 – 12 months, but there is no set rule.

It is quite usual for a sitter to seek several spiritual assessments with different mediums. Sometimes this is because they are still confused by what they have been given, and sometimes they want to hear something that has yet to be said. Others are looking to be 'discovered.'

We are all sensitive beings, and when we tread the pathway of spiritual development and professional work, we meet many well-meaning souls who give false hope. It's vital to keep your sitter as grounded as possible, as any potentials can also be ignored or rejected. Sometimes I liken it to proud parents who tell their children how they sing like pop stars and paint like a master, then feel devastated when they don't win the school prizes.

In spiritual work, there are many who will do the same as loving parents and tell you how amazing you are when you are still in the early stages of development. You are amazing anyway, but believing you are more experienced than you really are, leads to disappointment and will eventually serve as an injustice to your reputation and that other professionals. Some sitters are quite vulnerable, and we have a responsibility as mediums never to give false hope or unwise advice - especially when your working experience is limited and you haven't learned how to handle the vulnerability of others.

CONFUSING INFORMATION

As mediums and assessors, we are under pressure to deliver a successful and helpful assessment. Yet sometimes we hear the dreaded word 'no' despite what appears to us to be obvious information. It is easy to forget how the software and hardware of the mind work. Information is often received symbolically.

TIP: When you have clearly felt or seen information that is then refuted by the sitter, take a moment and simply describe what you saw, heard or sensed and leave it at that. Try not to analyse it too much. Simply offer it as the impressions you received – asking them to think about it all – then move on. Often, they know exactly what it means, and sometimes this information makes more sense later.

ATTEMPTS TO UNDERMINE

Sadly, some sitters (and luckily a tiny minority) try to take control and undermine the medium. Clearly, they have some other need than a genuine assessment. It usually manifests by:

• Constant dismissal of what you say

• Exaggerated praise of other teaching mediums appraisals of them

• Comments aimed at undermining you such as "all the other mediums were unavailable"

In all cases, if after the first few minutes you or the sitter are unhappy with the assessment, you can suggest bringing it to a close and offering a refund if they have paid for this time. Make this possibility clear before you start and then you both have an 'out' if it's not going well. After a few minutes of any sitting, asking your sitter if they are happy to continue is ideal.

NEVER DESTROY HOPE

Your words in a spiritual assessment have a wonderful capacity to heal, inspire, and empower. We must never give false hope, but at the same time, never destroy it. Most experienced spiritual assessors have sadly seen this happen and work hard to rebuild the destruction caused by another assessor, working too hard to please everyone.

I have a belief that we are all spirit and in being so worthy of an assessment. Not all of us are cut out for platform demonstration or professional work. However, we all have a valuable contribution to make. Assessors can be wrong at times and therefore, should not be stating someone should give up and have another career. There is skill in steering someone towards self awareness, that which makes them happy and fulfils a positive role. The key is never to believe you are the ultimate oracle on all things spiritual. Be open and look further when it's difficult to 'fit' someone into the usual spiritual roles you are aware of.

. . .

Some years ago, I was teaching a group for a week. It was a small group, and they became very closely bonded. We had such an incredible week, and the support was special to experience.

In this group was a consultant emergency doctor. She was new to developing mediumship but wanted to explore further. Although she looked very young for her age, her experience, knowledge and skills had saved many lives. Her mediumship ability was incredible! When she linked to spirit the room filled with a powerful energy and her evidence of spirit was accurate and advanced.

On the last day of the course, she had booked an assessment with one of my colleagues. She came back to class in tears and my colleague had told her she would never be any good at mediumship and should focus on getting a nice little job and settling down with a man. Little did my colleague know that this was the one person we want when our health is in danger and that also she was a brilliant medium. I can only assume my colleague was extremely tired at the end of a teaching week and took her eye off the ball for this assessment. The lesson here is to be honest and if you aren't up to working, don't!

The damage was done, and she never returned to study mediumship, because she had lost her trust in those who teach it. I am still disturbed all these years later that this happened.

RECORDING ASSESSMENTS

Some people do like to record their assessments. It's difficult to remember everything and now and again, a former sitter emails me to say they listened to their recording again and really enjoyed it.

. . .

I don't offer a recording facility, but if a sitter wishes to record it on their phone, they are welcome. However, I make sure they understand it is their responsibility, confidential and must never be shared, changed or posted online. So far everyone has honoured this.

A JOURNEY OF A SPIRITUAL
ASSESSMENT

E ach medium will with time find their own way of
working. Each medium may discover that every spiritual
assessment takes on its own organic format. This is
normal and reflects how unique each occasion and journey is.

However, when honing the skills of the spiritual assessment, it is
helpful to have a system to practice with, until the medium feels
confident to work organically and in their own style.

The system outlined below as a mind map can also be applied to
specific aspects of a spiritual assessment. You may also add or skip
any aspects if you wish. What matters is that if you know and
practice a system, once you develop your own style, you will have
broadened your approach, tried new ideas and increased your
skillset. The toughest part of any sitting is not knowing where to
start and where to go next, and the mind map will guide you, until
you establish your unique method of assessing.

I'm a big fan of mind maps. It's like the game I played with my
siblings on long car journeys. One starts a story and then hands
over to the next to add more and so on. None of us know how the

story will end and what will happen next. That's the beauty of the spiritual assessment. It's a true story that is being written every moment.

What follows is a mind map of areas that can be explored in the assessment. We will go through each aspect in turn in a clockwise direction, beginning with 'first energetic impressions'

SPIRITUAL ASSESSMENT MIND MAP

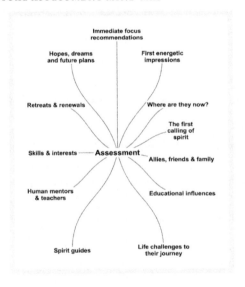

FIRST ENERGETIC IMPRESSIONS

Assuming we are prepared for the assessment - intention set, room ready etc. we are prepared to welcome our sitter. In the first moments, we naturally form some impressions such as

- Whether they appear friendly?
- Nervous?
- Suspicious?
- Excited?
- Relaxed?
- Confrontational?
- Sceptical?
- Engaging?
- Emotional?

. . .

These impressions must not cloud the actual assessment, but may guide us into the introduction, as we attune to the sitter. Ideally, our aim is for them to be as relaxed and as engaging as possible before we start.

Always begin with a friendly welcome, introducing yourself if you haven't met before and invite them to sit. A little 'small talk' such as 'the state of the weather' is often helpful and begins to establish a rapport. Ask if they need anything such as water and make it clear they can ask you to pause, stop and ask questions. This helps them feel in control of their choice to book an assessment with you and may calm any nerves or excitement.

After explaining what to expect, how you work and that you will leave some time for any questions at the end, it's time to attune to them spiritually. You will need to ask them if they wish to focus on a specific area or is a general assessment required. Whatever they choose, the mind map guide can apply to a general assessment and also a more specific area.

We covered attunement in chapter 2 and for some this is almost instant - for others taking a few moments to attune is important. Remember your method is right for you, but be brave and practice other ways too. You may need to be flexible in your approach if you find it hard to make an energetic link to your sitter. Never be afraid to say that you need a few moments to attune.

Your awareness of the sitter's energy needs to shift to the context of spiritual development. The mind map will guide you in many ways, but the first energetic impressions will start the assessment and strengthen the attunement.

First, describe to them what you sense initially, what you are shown, know, hear etc in relation to their current spiritual energy. Be open to areas outside of your experience and knowledge and if they arent clear, just share your impressions.

As an example; I often meet sitters who work with angels, dragons, unicorns and other areas I have not explored. Yet my psychic senses have never let me down, and when I have clairvoyantly seen evidence of their interest in these subjects, I say it. So far, so good. Be open to areas of discovery that you are unfamiliar with and also any areas you don't believe in yourself. Someone else's truth is their pathway, and we must not impose our own ideals and beliefs on their assessment.

Also, become aware of what their energy feels like if you are sensitive to this. I have learned with experience to sense a unique atmosphere if my sitter is a powerful healer, as opposed to a demonstrating medium.

Now you have the initial impressions and the sitter is ready , you can move on to where their development is now.

WHERE ARE THEY NOW?

It would be easy to assume that your sitter is at a crossroads and looking for solutions. This is possible and frequently the reason someone seeks a spiritual assessment. However, many are on their pathway of development and perfectly happy to let it unfold naturally and with no expectation.

Others need validation and some are seeking tangible solutions, whilst others just like a bit of time talking about their experiences.

Establishing where their current focus is, may become the key to the next steps they may choose to take. In addition, the starting point of the here and now, establishes a context for all the areas you are about to explore with your sitter.

In your attunement with them, again put the intention on the here and now and describe what you feel, see, sense, hear, know, etc. I repeat this advice from earlier, because if you get this right, the rest of the assessment often flows smoothly. If you get it wrong, self check you aren't being influenced by anything else in your mind, go back to the issue and if it's the same, just present it as 'this is what I sense right now - in this moment.' You can always ask them to bear it in mind for now. Remember, this isn't an evidential sitting - yet you need some acknowledgement for validating your information. If ultimately, your information is rejected - you can move on to another aspect and return to the 'now' later. By which time, it may well be clearer for both you and the sitter.

If you need a reminder or something to get your psychic impressions into focus for the assessment, you can revisit the mind map below and let your intuition guide you to what areas stand out and explore them with your sitter in the context of where they are now:

Sometimes you and your sitter need to think beyond the obvious and I share this example:

Many years ago, when I had first started working publicly with my mediumship, a highly respected medium told me I was a powerful healer. It rather surprised me as my focus was on evidential mediumship and it was going very well. I was in demand, and my accuracy was pretty high at the time. Not that I didn't feel like I was a healer (I had studied healing and worked many times with it) - I was just surprised that the medium mentioned this over the evidential mediumship and as a result I wrongly said "I can't take that."

Later, she asked me to stay behind when everyone was leaving. "I think you have a message from spirit for me" she said. I was taken aback, but spoke as I received impressions from the spirit world. The message was from her husband in spirit and was focussed upon acknowledging that he knew she had lost the bond of love between husband and wife, in his last years; yet he was grateful that she still looked after him, and she did so willingly as a good friend. Tears streamed down her face and she told me how grateful she was to hear this. She had always worried he felt a burden to her, and yet it had been her choice to care for him. She may not have been in love with him anymore, but she wanted to help him and enjoyed what became a beautiful friendship and trust between them.

"Thats your healing speaking" she told me. "You can heal through your mediumship as much as any other way." She left with a smile - it took me a while to process this, but the lesson was that she saw something in me that could heal and allowed me to discover the genuine power of it in what I was focussed upon. Ask your sitter to keep an open mind to information.

* * *

THE FIRST CALLINGS OF SPIRIT

I t is wondrous to take the mind back to the first callings of spirit. Perhaps we remember everything, or we forgot. Whilst others will have no memory of any spirit activity or experience of spirit or psychic activity as a child.

To a child, spirit phenomena are often a natural reality, uncluttered by doubts and the dismissive reasoning of adults. Adults may explain spirit phenomena as imagination - often through attempts to protect their child from fear, or possibly because they don't simply don't believe it to be spirit..

Yet most genuine childhood spiritual experiences are not scary, until children are told they are, or that they are 'bad' for repeating their experiences. Bedtime fairy stories - the tales created to teach us a moral code, often depict the unseen as something to be feared.

I remember by mother scolding me for telling my younger sister that an old woman sat on my bed at night and chatted to me. Yet it was true for most nights until I reached school age - when the visits stopped. Sometimes the old woman said nothing and carried on crocheting. Other times she talked - but I can't remember what she said now. Yet I can see her so clearly and describe her clothes in detail.

I also had two very good spirit friends who were real too. These were Jimmy (a boy of around 16) and Mrs Jurns (a lady in her fifties). I was so adamant they were there, that places for them were set at the table to placate me.

In addition, I often heard someone calling my name, yet nobody was there when I turned around. That lasted into my early school years, and several friends received the wrath of my tongue for playing tricks on me - yet they were innocent!

My mother was very psychic and saw spirit herself. Every year she did the cards for us and was mostly accurate. She also experienced spirit people in our house, including a man dressed in a top hat and wearing a wedding suit, who would walk around her bed and smile at her. Yet, she wouldn't bring herself to admit to me that my spirit friends were just as real. It's a parent's instinct to protect us from what frightens us. Except they didn't frighten me.

Years later, as an 18-year-old drama student in London, my flatmate had the idea to see a medium and wanted me to come. We found somewhere called the 'The World Spiritualist Mission' near Notting Hill Gate. From the tube station, we took a short walk and stepped into a large Georgian building that had a reception area selling books.

Behind the reception counter was a young woman who asked if she could help us. We asked if it was possible to see a medium. We had no idea you had to book an appointment, of course, but she was very kind and said wait a moment I will see if one of our resident mediums is free. She didn't want or ask for our names or any other details about us.

After a few minutes she said we could see Christina Burnett - Smith. She guided us next door to another house and we were asked to wait in a small sitting room. A tiny, elderly lady arrived and welcomed us, asking if we would join her for a pot of tea. She asked us to pull the curtains a little, whilst she made the tea, so she could see our aura's better. Then she returned with a tray of tea & biscuits, rattling the tea tray, just like Mrs Overall from the tv comedy Acorn Antiques!

Once we got started, Christina described in great detail about the elderly lady on the end of my bed, my childhood friendship with Jimmy and Mrs Jurns and also hearing my name being called from spirit. She also told me of a relative I had no idea about who was shot down in his plane, over Russia in the Second World War, and was now buried in Stuttgart, Germany. There were many more specifics that astounded me, and my mother validated that her cousin Charlie was the pilot, when I called her that evening.

It was a 'mind blowing' experience and the rest of our afternoon with Christina was spent discussing Spiritualism and some interesting physical mediumship relating to apports, she was involved with at the College of Psychic Studies in South Kensington.

She refused any money for this sitting, but welcomed us anytime to come and see her work either at the churches she served, or at the college. Sadly, we were so busy at drama school that we never saw her again. I often think about her.

For the first time, someone who didn't know me validated my childhood spiritual experiences and spirit friends with exceptional accuracy and triggered a renewed interest in spiritual education.

In your own work on spiritual assessments, you have the ability to validate the past experiences that led to your sitter's pathway of spiritual development. It is an incredibly empowering experience for any sitter. It validates their journey and may actually heal that memory that was denied or kept secret for years.

Using your psychic senses, look deep into that aspect of your sitter's life and allow whatever, wisdom, knowledge, images, or experiences to become known to you. It could be that your sitter can't remember. However, let them know what you sense and leave it with them to consider later if they wish.

Not all of us will have the same experiences of course, so again, work with what arises naturally and try not to fall into the trap that as children we experienced the same things. Many of us did, but whatever you receive, ask the spirit to validate it with something specific to the sitter.

I did experience a sitter who also had an elderly lady sitting on the end of her bed talking to her. So I doubted the information and assumed it was coming from my own subconscious mind. Then as I was about to dismiss it, she showed me from spirit, a jewellery box inlaid with mother-of-pearl with two initials on it. Once I relayed this, my sitter confirmed its validity and the two initial were the name of her elderly spirit visitor - her grandmother.

TIP: From time to time, look back at the exercise you completed in Chapter 1. Remind yourself of all your early experiences and add more if you later remember them. The more you explore these areas in your life, the more you can find for others. It's a 'psychic muscle' that requires exercise to become stronger.

EDUCATIONAL INFLUENCES

BEFORE WE WERE BORN

E ssentially, our first teachings come from the spirit. We are born into this life with a soul journey and it would make sense that although we often think of a newborn child as a 'blank slate' - It is merely the earthy experiences they are lacking.

Once a child can express themselves through language, many parents are astounded by the glimpses of wisdom and knowledge that are often spoken. The question arises whether we bring into this life a reservoir of knowledge and many examples exist which would suggest this could be the case.

In 2015, Dr Wayne W Dyer & Dee Garnes published with Hay House, a book entitled 'Memories Of Heaven.' The book is a collection of genuine stories about children who 'chose' their parents and includes many accounts of their experiences, prior to birth and their reason for 'choosing' their parents. Some accounts are incredible and include knowledge of ancestors they met before in the spirit realms, yet wouldn't have known about at the time of revealing this knowledge. In some examples, the parents had to research their family trees to discover who they were talking about, and it often turned out to be accurate!

Therefore, if this 'out of the mouth of babes' theory is true, we can assume that a consciousness and reasoning began before we were born and our education started in the spirit realms.

As most children forget theses accounts as they reach school age, it is hard to verify and validate. Thus, it will be wise to focus on that which your sitter can currently validate, but interesting to discover if any spiritual aspirations are impressed upon them, in this regard.

I often tend not to go back this far as it limits time and the validation aspect is troublesome. You will find sitters who would believe you if you told them they were the incarnation of Julius Caesar, such is their respect for your opinion. We are not in the business of giving false hope. Therefore, sticking to what we can validate is the ideal and the most helpful for future progress. I leave the prior to birth knowledge to those experts who specialise in past life regression.

EARLY EDUCATION

Much influence on the sitter's formative years will depend on the books they read, the films they watched, and the influences of family members. Tales of magical wizards, genie's & fairies who grant your wishes, dragons you can fly with and so much more are great wonders to children. Yet, all allow the mind an adventure into the realms of the seemingly invisible.

We still love these adventures as adults. Books and films such as the Harry Potter series are as much a delight for many adults as children. It is no coincidence that The Arthur Findlay College is affectionately called 'Hogwarts' by many students and staff, after the school for magicians, in J.K Rowling's novels.

Some children have been raised very spiritually and in families and traditions that believe in the spirit world, life after death and openly talk about this to their children. Whilst others will deny or shield the young mind. There is a threshold that is breached, when we understand we are mortal and physical life is not the eternal playground we took for granted.

If you are not so time limited, exploring the early influences of a sitter is to delve into a magical world and a world of awe and wonder. Later influences usually refine to more complex issues of 'life after death' and psychic phenomena.

INTENTIONAL EDUCATION

For many sitters there comes a point when they embrace learning about the spiritual aspects of life. At this point the assessor may look to the influences of:

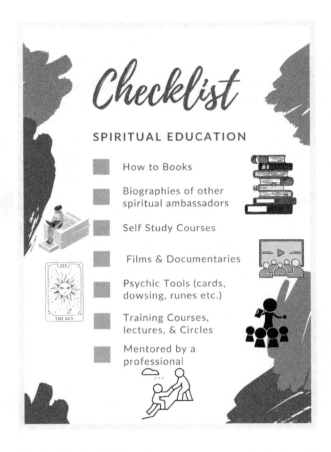

Checklist

SPIRITUAL EDUCATION

- How to Books
- Biographies of other spiritual ambassadors
- Self Study Courses
- Films & Documentaries
- Psychic Tools (cards, dowsing, runes etc.)
- Training Courses, lectures, & Circles
- Mentored by a professional

The checklist is a helpful guide to areas you can explore further. Of course it isn't just a matter of stating the sitter read books, watched films and took some courses. The skilled assessor will work with their own psychic senses to discover what type of books, films, course they etc. they explored and how they assisted them on their spiritual journey.

I remember a time when I had no access to the internet and relied upon the library and bookshops to discover more about developing my mediumship. I read everything I could find and some biographies of media mediums too. I learned a great deal and I also learned from those whose work I felt was poor quality. It helped me to discern what was right for me.

Therefore, when you explore the educational aspect of your sitter, also delve into:

• How they felt about it?

• What they learned?

• Did they continue learning from the same source or school of thought?

• Or did they move forward in another direction?

You just never know - it just may be the child who remembers life before life that educated them too.

* * *

CHALLENGES TO THE JOURNEY

PERSONAL CHALLENGES

The focus from early life moves from living in the present moment with the magical mind of the child, to what are we going to 'be' when we grow up. A famous quote that has been attributed to John Lennon is often posted on social media:

"When I was 5 years old, my mother always told me that happiness was the key to life. When I went to school, they asked me what I wanted to be when I grew up. I wrote down 'happy'. They told me I didn't understand the assignment, and I told them they didn't understand life."

Throughout education, it is encouraged that we our potential and then we will have choice as to what to 'be' one day. Our parents or guardians are concerned for us naturally and it would be unusual for a child to announce that when they grow up they want to be a medium, psychic, astrologer, tarot reader, spiritual healer etc.

Those early and possibly innate senses that were awakened in the early years wane and make way for the more traditional lifestyle expected of us as adults.

This is true of myself too. From childhood spirit friends, I later developed education aspirations, sporting hobbies and human friends who showed no interest in spiritual subjects, other than the church youth club. My ability to publicly express character, led me into theatre studies and then later, community social work, academia and finally a realisation that my truest calling was to share all I had learned, work with the spirit and teach.

There comes a time when you can't ignore what is your true calling and for me it emerged in my late twenties. However, although that was the start of the professional journey with spirit, I believe that we need to go through many challenges ourselves before we can truly represent the sacred work of the spirit. At 19, I would not have had the empathy and deep respect I now have for the journey of others and what life and death have challenged them with. It is rare to see very young mediums - not unknown but rare and I believe that you do need to experience and process many challenges in your own life in order to understand and respect the journey of your sitter.

However, there were many challenges. First, my academic colleagues were scathing if anything remotely spiritual was spoken of. Second, came ridicule from some family and friends, then there was the sense of not knowing how to get this all started and work with it and also, how would I survive financially if I didn't keep my regular job?

Many sitters often ask for the right time to give up work and dedicate their time to spiritual areas. My answer is "when the work gives you up". In other words, you are so busy and successfully supporting yourself in your spiritual endeavours, there is no time left for the regular work and not before. This is a precarious area of work, with no sick pay or pension. If you don't work, you won't earn a living.

When we explore the challenges in a sitter's journey, there may be several aspects that have impacted their choices and shaped their journey such as

• Prejudice and ridicule

• Family commitments

• Fear of the unknown

• Financial security

• Lacking self confidence

• Being told by someone you respected you would never be good enough

• Lack of support & encouragement

• Disability

• Underestimating your potential

• Overconfidence and not being as prepared as you thought you were

The list can be added to, of course, but these are commonly discovered in an assessment and exploring this with your intention, may help you unlock some challenging themes, so the sitter has something to work with for progress. It may also validate their journey so far and the issues that were present, have now been overcome, acknowledged and validated by you - the assessor.

PRACTICAL CHALLENGES

Facing many on the path of spiritual development are practical challenges. Already noted are family commitments and financial security. Yet there are other practical considerations such as somewhere you can study or conduct your work. You may not have a spare room or dedicated study area and unless you live alone, the chances are your study, work and spiritual practices are frequently interrupted.

For several years, online forums and teaching platforms for spiritual development have been successfully running. Many have discovered they can study from home when they have a quiet moment, participate, and assist their development. The barrier to this would be not having the technology such as a computer or tablet and a good internet connection. Hopefully, this is becoming rare in the western world, but if you live in a remote rural region, you may need to travel to a local internet cafe.

The barrier that could be holding someone back or have been a significant challenge in their development, could just be that issue of travel. Not everyone drives, has good public transport or someone who can help them get to where they need to be.

Never has there been so much teaching and online development available, and it is here to stay. The COVID-19 pandemic, resulted in many experienced teachers, having to work online because of travel restrictions. The choice of training is now extensive, with all levels of experience catered for. Teachers who shied away from online work are now committed to it and won't stop once they can travel again.

As long as we question everything, keep an open mind and be prepared to discover what is our own truth, other sources such as free webinars, YouTube and live classes on social media are in plentiful supply and can make a real difference.

Dedicated training time is often a challenge discovered by many. If a sitter holds down a full-time job, then annual leave to take a course of study may be impossible. This is especially true if the family depends on you to spend time with them.

From the assessors standpoint, some issues to explore with the
psychic senses, relating to the practical challenges faced by a sitter
(past or present):

• Space to work

• Technology if required

• Ability to travel

• Time

• Money

TRIBES AND TEACHERS

When we find a group of like-minded spiritual people we form
strong bonds of friendship. This happens online and in person. Yet
none of us develop at the same pace or in the same way. The
classes, circles and courses may all teach the same thing to our
group, yet we will all have a unique experience of them.

Seeing your friends achieve something you have worked towards
and not yet mastered is quite tough to cope with. You are pleased
for their success but sad about your own (even when your progress
is exactly where it needs to be at the time) Sometimes it even leads
to a sense of being left behind and leads to a spiritual worker giving
up on their spiritual pathway, or giving up on some friends.

Conversely, you may be the one storming ahead with new skills,
ready to show the world what you can do and feel you have less in
common with your former spiritual tribe. Maybe you need to be
challenged more than your current situation allows. Your friends
may feel rejected and although there is growth to be discovered on
all sides - it's a challenge to consider and one that many of us
experience.

There comes a time when you need to move on and make way for others. This is natural and marks a significant moment in your progress. We can try to hang on to what is our comfort zone, but in reality it is being outside the comfort zone that helps us in the long run. Moving on can be hard, but staying put and not progressing, can lead to stagnation.

Most of us can remember a teacher at school , who inspired us, believed in us, and who we respected. As adults and on our spiritual journey, we will meet many teachers. Whether it is through books, films, churches and centres, courses and circles - there are inspirational teachers everywhere. Including you!

During my early development, I read some really awful book on spiritual development and mediumship. They just didn't ring true for me, and some were just poor attempts to capitalise on a celebrity medium's popularity. Some probably weren't even written by the medium. However, I read as much as I could - even what I consider being rubbish and I believe it has helped me discern more. It has helped me value what is helpful, profound and educational or even purely sensational.

Those books taught me a lot, as did some courses I undertook. As I progressed and the opportunity arose, I attended a few courses in mediumship. My formative development was by myself, but there came a point when I was asked to work in churches and I needed to learn more skills. The first course I took was in a Spiritualist church and I understood nothing. The teachers were so unclear what the objectives were, and I felt lost. I also studied a few evenings in London with a brilliant teacher Anthony Kesner, and that helped me move forward with demonstrating mediumship. Later I attended a course with Glyn Edwards and Jill Harland at the Arthur Findlay College. I found their wisdom exceptional - Glyn and Jill became colleagues and friends later. Other courses led by well known mediums were not always as I expected and in some cases I didn't appreciate the bias and ego shown by some teachers. However, you consider this; it taught me that when I became a teacher, I would not follow their examples, yet I would value the excellent precedents set by the veritable experts who I aspired to. It was worthwhile experiencing this.

As a spiritual assessor, whether it is personal, practical, your tribe or your teachers that were challenges, this is an area where you really can discover, what brought your sitter to the point of where they are in the time they are with you. It will help you consolidate a forward plan for them and also appreciate their journey and contribution to the work they do.

Remember, challenges are not always negative, so also focus on the positive experiences - the successes too, such as when someone pushed through the barriers and came out the other side stronger and wiser.

* * *

GUIDES & MENTORS

SPIRIT GUIDES

There is a widely held belief in spiritual work that we have a spirit guide throughout our journey and many spiritual workers find great wisdom, guidance and reassurance from knowing and working with them. It is also believed that at certain times in our development, another guide may come forward to assist until they are no longer required. Yet, primarily, we have one main one.

One theory is that they are part of our soul group and part of a 'collective' consciousness that we can commune with.

Spirit guides are archetypes. They are the sages, the medicine men and women, the magicians, the crones, the tribal elders amongst many archetypes and our soul is assigned with the archetype it needs, for its journey.

There is a commonality found in 'guide' archetypes for example:

• Native American chiefs

- Aboriginal elders

- Monks, nuns, priests

- Maori & Maasai warriors

- The Herbalist in the woods

All nations and cultures have their wise teachers and mostly we discover spirit guides align with bringing necessary teachings, guidance and wisdom to the spiritual seeker. They assist us in learning important lessons and empower us to do this without us blindly following what we believe they are saying. It is as a wise parent would be.

Not everyone is aware of who their guide is and what archetype they represent. Some people never see or hear them, yet many are aware of a presence that guides them and trust their intuition as a sign their guide is by their side - so to speak. Interestingly, whether you know your guide by clairvoyance, clairaudience or any other sense, they tend to align with your own spiritual philosophy. As above, so below.

An aspect of the spiritual assessment is helpful if it can place some focus on this area. Whilst we don't wish to impose a spirit guide on someone who hasn't an awareness of them, we can attune to their energy and realise the guiding influences of the sitter's journey and offer our discoveries to them. Of course we can also describe, if we do happen to see a monk or a tribal chief etc and also if we receive any information about them.

However, the danger is influencing the sitter's mind and interfering with their own relationship with their spirit guide. Therefore, we should never correct them if they don't recognise the information, as it is their journey to discover - we can simply let them know what we sense and leave it at that. If well attuned to your sitter, it is rare they would not recognise the wise influences you have sensed.

Many years ago I was having dinner with a couple of friends at their house. Both were mediums and one told me my spirit guide was a certain Native American warrior and chief and told me his name. It wasn't one of the most well-known chiefs, but I could look up some history and discover it was a genuine person who had lived before.

I tried communing in my mediations with him, but nothing came back - nada. I also didn't feel or sense anything toward him. I read his story and all about his tribe, but deep inside I knew this had come from the mind of my friend and was not related to me. Once I came to this realisation, and dropped this well-meaning pretence of this personal guide, I felt free and my progress continued with a renewed sense of a different force that was guiding me. Since then, and many spiritual meetings with archetypes later, I only ask for their presence to be known. I know my spirit guide by their energy and presence and in my case, that's all I need.

In the spiritual assessment, validation of the spiritual, philosophical influences and resonances with a sitter is important to them and in a general assessment, this awareness should be spoken of. It can be one of the most significant pieces of information discovery that will give your sitter confidence that they are on the right path.

If your sitter is unaware, it's ok to talk about guides and guidance in terms of their qualities and without a title or culture. If they have a name - let the sitter find it. However, the name isn't as important as what they bring to the sitters progress.

On another aspect of working with guides, it's important to remember that a guide is specifically for the progress of the individual they are assigned to. It would not be correct to give an assessment to a sitter, stating information is from your spirit guide. Yours is for your journey and theirs is for them. Your guide has enough on their plate to assist you. The work of the spiritual assessment is within your skillset of psychic ability.

73

MENTORS

Throughout our journey there are many mentors we may meet along the pathway. Some are no longer alive in the physical world and left an incredible legacy, with their experiences of working with spirit. Others, are still alive and well and working in this life now. They are the inspirers that keep us moving forward, believe in us and help us thrive in our spiritual work.

Although they are not spirit guides, their inspirational role to us is significant. Most mentors have experienced all the dramas, the scepticism, the disappointments and the beauty of serving spirit and healing others.

In recent times, mentors have set up continuing education programmes for mediums. These are often either in person over several weekends or online, and offer the opportunity for a programme of study that is progressive and supportive. We can 'bumble' along picking and choosing different courses, but sometimes we find a teacher who resonates with our journey and a series of trainings with them is beneficial.

In my development, I didn't follow a pathway of working with a specific mentor. I consider many of my mentors are amongst, colleagues, friends and former students. Also, with great respect, those now in the spirit world who shared their wisdom are amongst the many I consider mentors.

One in particular who is now in spirit, asked prior to her passing if she could mentor me for inspirational speaking. Her ability for this was outstanding. I knew she would never be well enough to do this, and she passed a few months later. However, her legacy and her intention put her at the top of the list of mentors, as I often look to her work, dedication and ability as a source of great learning and inspiration.

There are many who seek the mentorship of someone who has a high profile in mediumship within the media. Many of these mediums are indeed a great credit to our work. What is sad is that some students wish to be associated with them merely to add to their list of associates and credentials, to create a presence for themselves? It doesn't matter who trained you, so much as how you work and represent your chosen field.

We honour our mentors and one day, many will look to your wisdom and experience as a source of quality spiritual development. If we put someone on a pedestal, one day they will topple and fall. For all mentors possess human fallibility too.

What is important for the developing spiritual worker, is that gratitude, grace and discernment are foremost in whether they are a part of our journey.

This aspect of your spiritual assessment is wonderful to explore. When I delve into this area, I often see books and images of past pioneers. It is very special and often brings me back to the roots of my own development and what I had forgotten.

When you explore the aspect of mentors also consider those who are currently mentoring others and if they have had any influences upon the sitter already.

You may be asked about recommending a mentor. It's important never to denigrate or disparage another mentor to a sitter. There is a teacher for everyone if needed and as a professional, it's important you respect that colleagues all have something special to share. If one or two stand out very positively, there is no harm in suggesting the sitter considers their teachings and leave it with them to decide.

* * *

YOUR SUPPORT NETWORK

In chapter 13 on 'challenges,' the subject of friends and peers during your development was considered. It isn't always a simple path and the friends we started our journey with, if we were in a group, will often drift in different directions - as will you. When everything appears to be harmonious it is difficult to imagine such changes, but they will inevitably happen and when they do, it's important to stay positive and wish them well too. Bitterness has no place in spiritual development other than causing angst, stress, and holding you back from your full potential.

Sadly, I have experienced many relationships break up as one partner cannot accept or believe in the spiritual journey of the other. Perhaps there were underlying problems as well, but it is true that not everyone will support you and a parting of ways is sometimes reported.

In this part of the spiritual assessment we can also look positively at those who are supportive or accepting of the sitter's development, despite differing beliefs or interests.

With the positive intention of support, it is exquisite to see the smile on the sitter when we explore their journey in the context of their support network. To assist this, we can separate it into areas such as

• Partners

• Friends

• Family

• Colleagues

• Teachers

• Fellow students

• Fellow professionals

• Children

• Living mentors

• Books

• Study courses

Although the journey may seem lonely for some, there are so many written resources, blogs, vlogs and courses with support groups, there is every chance your sitter will not feel so isolated when you explore this aspect for them. Sometimes, we need a boost and a reminder of the surrounding support.

* * *

SKILLS & INTERESTS

helendavita.com

R eferring to the graphic in chapter 4, this is the part of
the assessment that is very exciting and most times
enlightening for the sitter. Validating their skills and

interest is special, and we feel good when someone we respect and trust can see that each of us has ability.

As a spiritual assessor, it is positive to discover what another is skilled at. Sometimes those skills are latent and often the sitter is aware, but hasn't developed them as yet.

You can allow all your psychic faculties to go wild and deliver enthusiastically what your sitter is capable of. Remember, some have come to you feeling as if they should give up. It's true that the path of spiritual development is not for everyone, but for some, it's merely a case of having someone believe in you. When your sitter realises that they have relevant skills and interests, then they are in the best position to decide for themselves what to do with them!

Your awareness as a sitter will show many ways a particular skill can work for someone. Don't be surprised if you encounter a new and unusual approach.

Several years ago I was teaching a group of students at The Arthur Findlay College. It was a mixed ability group, and they were very enjoyable to work with. One particular student had saved for years to attend the college for this week, and as with all students, I wanted their week to make a positive difference for them.

From the beginning of the week, the student in question asked if she could practice her spirit art and that if we had to give readings to each other, could she draw spirit portraits instead? I confirmed with the group that this was a request and they were all delighted to support her.

As the week progressed, my spirit artist became more introverted and appeared unhappy. I took her aside after class and she told me she knew she could draw, but it just wasn't working this week. She requested an assessment so we could have specific time to look into this.

I began the assessment with a general overview as per the mind map and then moved my focus to the art. Clairvoyantly and very clearly I was being shown her not drawing, but sculpting. As I told her this, she was so excited as she loved sculpting. Yet, she had not regarded this as a possibility with her spiritual work. She promised she would attempt this when she was back at home.

For the rest of the week, she put away her pencils and paper and joined in the regular group exercises. After a few weeks, I received an email asking for my home address as she had something she wanted to send as a gift.

In due course, a parcel arrived and inside was a beautifully sculpted head and shoulders of my grandmother in spirit! Ever since, she has focussed upon evidential sittings and is in great demand for her sculptures of past family members.

When it comes to skills and interests, there are some questions you can ask yourself as an assessor:

• Is this a powerful skill or interest?

• Are they feeling positive about it?

• Is it something they have no interest in?

• How can they develop it further?

• Is there a specific or unique aspect of this they can expand upon?

• Who can help them develop it?

• What is their journey to discover this skill or interest?

• Has it been through any significant changes?

• Recommended books, courses and media

Some assessors will wish to begin their skills and interests assessment at the beginning of the sitting, and this is also acceptable. Remember the mind map is a guide and you can go through it all in order, pick and choose aspects, bypass some aspects and adapt as appropriate.

RETREAT & RESTORE

Therewill be times in our lives when we need a pause from what we are currently engaged with. Burn out is real and especially in spiritual development.

The more in demand you become, the more you travel with your work and lesser time spent honouring your need for rest, fun, family and friends - will contribute to the dreaded burn out. The possibility exists of giving up on something you once loved doing and brought great satisfaction and help to others.

As your work becomes popular, the critics and competitors increase and that in itself, can lead to a mental fatigue that needs care.

For spiritual assessors and those seeking their services, burn out is equally possible.

It is often a fine balancing act between turning down work and exhausting yourself, physically and mentally. Professional spiritual workers are self employed and losing work means losing income. However, there is another aspect that concerns those of us working in this field and that is reputation.

Many fear that if they say 'no' too many times to work, they will stop being asked. It's a genuine fear and an understandable situation. There are just so many times a person will accept a 'no' before they give up on you. We must find the key in finding a balance and a way to retreat and restore yourself to good mental and physical health as much as is possible.

When you are conducting a spiritual assessment, this is something to consider seriously in your sitter. You will need to delve into their energy, put aside the spiritual work and discover what else or where else, makes them happy, at peace, rest, feel in good health, also the people or animals that bring them back to a feeling of being reconnected and restored again. All this you can explore in their energy.

First, you may need to establish if they are looking after their personal time well and have achieved a healthy balance in life. I have always taught that whilst we may know the spirit world; we are living in this one now and meant to live it as fully as possible. I keep a mental note that when my time comes and I reach the spirit world, I could be met with exasperation for being blessed with a chance of wonderful physical life and ignoring it; when all those in spirit were perfectly fine without my dedication, anyway! Now my homelife comes first and there is plenty of time for spirit too.

Explore this aspect carefully and if all is in balance, then let your sitter know and move on. If not, then explore further as to what is being neglected.

With that intention, allow yourself to be shown or sense their life and work balance. Describe the images and feelings, (without doom and gloom). Be shown the people, places and animals that are missing their presence. Make gentle suggestions to redress the balance.

Many successful and busy spiritual workers have done this by setting their own rules such as

83

• No work on one particular day of the week - every week

• No more than 4 trips away from home a year

• Date nights and children's play dates once a week.

• No working after 8pm

• Take at least a two-week break every year and honour family and religious celebrations

These are just some examples, and there will be many more to explore and suggest. A day here and there, away from spiritual work always helps when overwhelmed, but sometimes a longer break is recommended and as part of the assessment it is something to consider and share sensitively, if you can see that the dreaded burn out is on the horizon.

* * *

HOPES, DREAMS & FUTURE PLANS

W hen we come to this stage of the spiritual assessment, the work is more conversational. Whilst as an assessor, you can attempt to sense as much as possible, it is good practice to allow your sitter time to ask you some questions.

Bearing in mind that by this time, they have had a significant focus on what you as the expert have discovered about them and how they are fulfilling their journey. It is now time for them and the questions that will assist you with making a plan, or suggesting further training. This can often be summarised by discussing what their future needs and desires appear to be from the assessment and what your sitter is hoping to achieve.

Remember this is primarily the sitter's opportunity to talk about what they wish for in the future, so just ask the question - where do you want to go from here with your spiritual work?

It's very possible they will say they need some time to process all the information in the sitting and have a think about it. That's a superb thing to do and is a measure that they have taken the assessment seriously and will give time to their considerations.

You are by now both winding down from all the psychic energy that has been flowing and bringing yourselves back to the present moment.

RECOMMENDATIONS

By this point, you as an assessor have a very good idea about the abilities, the hopes and dreams, the experiences, their guides and mentors and many other aspects of the sitter's spiritual pathway.

I am a great believer in trying to do one thing well as opposed to doing lots of things half heartedly or with little depth. It's a simple concept of teaching that if you take one subject and explore it thoroughly, you will reach a greater critical mass of learning than if you try to teach too many subjects together.

With this philosophy in mind, at this point the sitting is almost over and the ideal question is:

"If you could only work on one thing related to your spiritual development, what would it be?"

Asking this question focusses the mind of the sitter to discover what is most important to them. If you can help them with this, they gain the confidence to tackle any other issues that have preoccupied their minds.

Whatever, the answer is think for moment:

• Do they need some specific coaching to help them?

• If so, who is an expert in this field?

• What courses (online, residential or postal) are available that would help them?

• Are there any exercises or meditations they can do themselves at home to help?

• Would they benefit from a mentoring programme?

• What educational resources would you suggest to them?

Having reached the end of the assessment - it is time to thank them and wish them well. The good work is now done and now time for both the sitter and the spiritual assessor to retreat and restore - until it's time for more good work.

GLOSSARY

1. Apports: objects that materialise in a seance room from elsewhere
2. Arthur Findlay College (AFC): A world renowned Spiritualist college of psychic sciences
3. Attunement: relates to a state of energetic spiritual harmony
4. Evidential medium: Someone who communicates with the deceased and provides evidence of their continued existence
5. Psychic medium: The psychic medium is someone who interprets the energy of a living being or earthly object and communicates the impressions received through their senses.
6. Objective clairvoyance: experiencing as if the vision is physically present
7. Sitter: A person/client receiving a 'sitting' with an intuitive/psychic/evidential medium
8. Sitting: a meeting between a medium and a sitter

9. Subjectively clairvoyant: experiencing the vision within the mind
10. Spirit guide - a spiritual archetype assigned only to you, to assist your spiritual progress

ABOUT THE AUTHOR

Helen DaVita is the Principal of Eagle Lodge Training and is also an approved training provider. She carries over 30 years of wisdom as a universal spiritual teacher & inspirational speaker, world-renowned Intuitive, Arthur Findlay College Tutor and sentient Animal Communicator. Helen is likewise a leading educator of being in altered states and trance mediumship.

Helen's belief, is that we are all 'one' - one universe, one nature, one family and that spiritual development must be in harmony to be authentic. Authenticity is found in a type of 'permaculture' of the spirit. Each aspect has a purpose, and it must not be divisive or create a separation. It must encompass nature, animals and energy. It is the way our ancient ancestors knew to survive and has no religion.

helendavita.com

ACKNOWLEDGMENTS

The Power of Spirit

Printed in Great Britain
by Amazon

40578688R00066